THE OTHER SIDE OF THE COIN

Benefits of vitality leadership

First Edition

Chad D. Bumgarner

ISBN: 1537096907
ISBN-13: 978-1537096902

DEDICATION

To my wife and my three daughters who are so loving and patient with me! Thank you for your support, strength and love. You allow me to live out my passion which is to serve and help create generations of leaders who will help make tomorrow a better world to live in! Everything that I do is for you guys!

ACKNOWLEDGEMENTS

First of all, I would like to thank God for placing the right mentors and coaches in my life so that I can do what I do with impact, passion and love.

I'm really excited to be writing this book because it wouldn't have come to fruition if it hadn't been for my coach, A.M. Williams pushing me and helping me to see things in me that I've never seen before! Thanks coach!

I would like to thank my entire Bumgarner family for your constant support and encouragement. I know I'm not the easiest person to love but I thank God for each and every one of you!

Thanks to my mentors: Dr. John L. Mason and Dr. Thomas Kail. I would also like to thank Rhonda Sherrod, Penny Rolle, Dr. Betsy Johnson, Kenya Rutland, The National Society of Leadership and Success. Last but not least, my mother and father, Mr. & Mrs. L. Douglas Bumgarner.

THIS PAGE IS LEFT BLANK ON PURPOSE

INTRODUCTION

Take some time to reflect on your life and your leadership role regardless of its' capacity. What would it take for you to get to the next level? What would it take for you to live the life that you've always wanted to live? What do you feel are the road blocks and setbacks that are keeping you from living your desired life and leading in a way that makes you almost irreplaceable? The next chance you get, stand in front of a mirror and get completely honest with yourself and ask this one question. Is my leadership life-giving or is it life-taking?

In other words, am I adding value to my team and my company by how I lead? Am I grooming new leaders for the future and empowering others to constantly learn, grow and improve? Am I breathing life into a stale and stagnant environment while working on enhancing the culture that's keeping it in the stone ages?

Or, am I the reason why we aren't growing? Maybe I'm the reason why our retention rate is extremely low along with the morale. These are just a few of the questions that you need to ask yourself in order to see where you stack up. Success and failure rises and sets on the leadership that is in place. John Maxwell says that constantly and I'm a firm believer in that as well

Often times leaders find it so challenging to lead others. There are so many dynamics in play along with the many different and unique personalities, policies and procedures that leaders have to deal with on a daily basis. I believe that the one reason why so many leaders struggle is because they lack balance.

They lack balance because they only focus one side of leadership. *There are two sides to leadership, the functional side and the vitality side.* The functional side is by far the most recognized and talked about side. However, the vitality side is like the "black sheep" of the family but amazingly enough, it's probably just as important if not, the most important side to leadership there is.

In order to enjoy life and enjoy what you do, there should be some kind of balance. Most leaders when successful, have people under them that are just as successful. What's missing in your leadership? Is it interpersonal skills? Lack of effective communication? The way you reach people has to become infectious and addictive.

You, as a leader set the tone so how you work with others will hopefully rub off on everyone else around (in a positive manner, obviously) and eventually create an environment that is healthy and vibrant. If you would incorporate some vitality into your equation, you will surely be able to reap the benefits (fun, freedom, flexibility & fulfillment) from it and you will see how much better your leadership will become and how much better your life will thrive!

With vitality leadership you not only get what you want, the team should also get the same things. Imagine how much more productive and effective a team could be when they realize that they can have the fun, freedom, flexibility & fulfillment that you have!

CONTENTS

PHOTO CREDITS:

JHardman Photography: pg.76
John Q. Adams quote from : brainyquote.com

What is leadership?

This question has long been a debated one because arguably there is no one right answer to this loaded question. The range of answers cover the full spectrum of possibilities and what it could be. For example, one definition could be that leadership is the ability to bring people together to achieve a common cause. Another could be that leadership is simply influence. As you can see, the range is broad but neither are wrong. Leadership is definitely dynamic and multi-dimensional in the aspect of the kinds and types of leaders as well as how to be an effective leader.

Leadership from the dynamic side of things is basically understanding what approach to use in your leadership position. This thoroughly depends upon what you're trying to accomplish, what your time table looks like, how organized or unorganized the existing environment is, etc. For example, if you are in the office and all of a sudden a fire breaks out and people are screaming and panicking and there's chaos all around, you would need to turn into an authoritative leader. An authoritative leader takes control of a situation and proceeds to give orders for everyone to follow. This isn't the time for Q&A. Leaders in this mind frame are not looking for conversations, input or feedback. They just want you to do what they are commanding so that everyone can be safe and get out alive.

The dynamics can really be frustrating and sometimes confusing if you aren't used to it or are not very familiar with it. There will be times when a leader will have to switch their approach several times a day depending on what the situation calls for and what approach they feel will have the most impact. There are leaders that will have to go from transformational to charismatic. In other words, in one situation you may have to be empathetic and have high emotional intelligence to deal with people. On the other hand, you may have to shift into the transactional leader whereas you will need to clarify roles and responsibilities and judge your team members based on performance.

The multi-dimensional side comes in and it's just as important to leadership. People love to see and follow leaders who are able to be multi-dimensional. Most people want leaders to have integrity. If you made a mistake, own it! People really connect with leaders who make themselves vulnerable to a point. One of the biggest selling points with successful leaders is that they make everyone feel as though they can be trusted. You have to understand that gaining and keeping someone's trust is often times hard to do. However, being able to do it will speak volumes about you and your ability to lead and effectively connect with people.

Another multi-dimensional side of leadership is sociability. Leaders need to be able to friendly, outgoing, diplomatic and establish strong, healthy social relationships. Leaders that have the ability to be sociable also show confidence while bringing positive energy to the situation or the conversation. Along with sociability, people like leaders to be focused and driven to accomplish what they set out to accomplish. Leaders with passion are contagious and that creates a catalyst for success while increasing followers at the same time.

What I've just given you was just a glimpse of what leadership can be and how it could be. There are many, many more traits, attributes, characteristics, and thoughts about what leadership is and what it should be. Leadership is broad and can often be very vague. Leadership is ever-evolving and we need to be prepared to evolve as well. However, no matter how many times or ways we look at this topic, we all execute it in different ways. We perform, implement and discuss leadership in one way and one way only. That one way we do this, is functionally. Most leaders are functional and we all at one point have it or will have it down to a science.

Leadership is more than just functional but we can't see the forest for the trees! This side of leadership is the most popular and most talked about and studied portion of leadership. Nonetheless, there is another side to it that no one ever speaks about. This side, if studied and practiced, can help you become a leader among leaders. It will give you more balance, respect, clarity, and the ability and opportunity to live life to the fullest and lead your team more effectively. This side of leadership is called vitality leadership and you'll read more about this later on in the book.

THE OTHER SIDE OF LEADERSHIP

Functional Leadership

There are two sides to every coin and for every action there is an equal or opposite reaction. Most people either don't realize this or understand it but it's no different with leadership. The one side that we know the most about and are familiar with is the functional side. This is the side that we've been taught and it's also the side that we see the most of. The functional side of leadership is the side that's always serious, stern and predictive. People like this do their job and go through the motions with their check lists.....uh, I mean their department or division's quarterly goals or initiatives. This is the epitome of functional.

Years ago I used to work as a contractor for this agency in the health and human services industry. We were a group of contractors working on an international website with the sole purpose of keeping it updated and online 24/7 365. Our program director was a leader who knew all too well about the functional side of leadership.
As I said earlier, some leaders are life-giving and others are life-taking.

In other words, some leaders energize their people and environment. They find ways to breathe life into everything that they do and everyone they work with. They are able to break down situations and help others see the importance of what they do and why it's important for us to do what we do. Well, my director was the exact opposite.

Our director was stiff and his communication with the team was toxic. It was more of a military environment whereas the communication was one way. He would enter meetings and inform us on what needed to be done and what quarterly goal it was linked to. This is how he ran his department for 8yrs and it sucked the life right out of it. The turnover rate was ridiculous and being that we worked in a data center, we needed qualified engineers to network and configure servers as well as install and setup unique applications. The director

9

focused only on the quarterly goals that we needed to hit. There was no life in the environment. Most people were working but didn't know why they were doing what they were doing. We all just focused on one project after another. Imagine doing that day in and day out year after year. Some of you are probably doing it now!

In all honesty, it's probably not my former director's fault. More than likely he was taught that way. A lot of us are. As leaders most of us are taught to dot the I's and cross the T's and that's actually not a bad thing. However, as we all know, leadership is not a one-way street. It isn't one dimensional.

Learning just one aspect of leadership, the functional side, can eventually erode and deteriorate a team or an organization. It can also cause unnecessary stress to the team or the environment thus causing potential anxiety to some people. It's just not healthy to the environment as a whole much less the individuals that make up the team in the environment.

The program manager in this case (like most other leaders) more than likely got promoted into this area because of their great work in the position before this one. They could have been very good at their job. However, this is also a huge mistake that a lot of senior leadership members make. They find someone who's great at their job and then promote them only to find later that the promotion was not a good idea and the impact was not what they were hoping for. Please understand, just because someone is good at their job DOES NOT mean that they are good at managing or leading people. I experienced this first hand with the program manager and also with a team mate of mine.

My teammate was an exceptional engineer. He was bright, knowledgeable and very resourceful. He eventually found favor in the eyes of senior leadership and was eventually promoted to the manager of the engineering department. It didn't take long to see that this move wasn't a good one. He constantly clashed with the engineering team and completely distanced himself from the team altogether. He wasn't really good with communication other than making requests and demands about what he wanted done. It got to the point where what little trust he had with the team had quickly deteriorated. Engineers were leaving about as fast as they were coming in the door! Everything was always the team's fault so there was no accountability. He literally just sucked the life out of the department. There was no more fun in the office and he removed the flexibility altogether with the elimination of working from home once a week and having fixed schedules. He didn't trust anyone and his communication in meetings and on conference calls were calculated, cold and sharp.

This guy struggled severely with emotional intelligence but refused to see the error of his ways until it almost cost him the entire engineering team. The team had ultimately had enough and went to senior leadership and demanded that this person be removed or they were going to quit. This is a prime example of functional leadership (a bit extreme but nonetheless a good example) at its' best. A person that's good at what they do, but not so good at leading people.

 I got the opportunity to catch up with him years later at company function. I had moved on to another job elsewhere but was invited to this event. When I saw him, I greeted him and asked how things were. Let me just say that he has come a long way and is now supposedly a better leader than years ago. I was happy to hear that he learned why his leadership wasn't where it should have been back then.

Functional leadership is a necessary one but as with all things that are good or successful, balance is the key. What are you bringing to the table as a leader? How are you going to not only get things done, but also breathe life into a dead scene or culture? Vitality is the missing ingredient that most leaders really need in their leadership toolbox. We have to learn to be a life source to our team or environment. Happy and engaged employees equal higher productivity, a positive morale in the department, and better working relationships. All of this happens when a leader understands and exudes vitality.

When most leaders lead with only the functional side, they are unknowingly divorcing themselves from leadership balance. Functionality and vitality are like ying and yang. You shouldn't have one without the other. Unfortunately, a lot of leaders either don't know about the vitality side, or just refuse to incorporate it into their leadership strategy. When this happens, you can rest assure that there will potentially be no life in that environment and employees WILL end up leaving for better opportunities..........and leadership!

QUESTIONS FOR INSIGHT

1. After reading this, how do you feel about your leadership and its' effectiveness on those around you?

   _____

   _____

   _____

   _____

2. Do you feel that emotional intelligence is something that your team and leadership can benefit from? Why?

   _____

   _____

   _____

   _____

Benefits of vitality leadership

THE OTHER SIDE OF LEADERSHIP

VITALITY LEADERSHIP

Congratulations!! You have just taken the red pill! Before we go into vitality and the benefits of it, we must understand what exactly vitality is. Vitality means to be strong or to give continuance of life to something. It means being active and having energy. How many of us would like to be a bit stronger in every since of the word and have energy in our lives? Now, most of us have jobs and work for someone and yet a few others have their own businesses with employees. The average American spends quite a bit of time at work on a daily basis so leisure time has almost completely taken a back seat to progress and success.

Most of us work a job because we have to in order to provide for our lifestyle and other things that we may want to acquire. Many of us on a daily basis wonder or often think about how we can become better at what we do or how we can get a promotion. There's nothing wrong with that if that's all you are looking for. However, what if I told you that success for you usually comes when you work to grow and build others. If you can empower and enhance the people around you with vitality leadership skills, what does that say about you and what you're able to do?

Vitality leadership is such a huge aspect of a leader because it shows another side……..a human side which for many employees is simply unheard of! For many years leaders have isolated themselves from their group only to find later that they are truly disconnected from reality. Vitality leadership means finding a way to resurrect "life" into an environment or an organization. It means pouring into others and helping them to achieve as well as advance if they so choose to. It means uplifting the teams or departments and giving them a shot in the arm of enthusiasm! Our job is to encourage and inspire because after all, we are leaders right? We have to find ways to keep our teams engaged, equipped, lively and informed. We want to keep the turnover rate as low as possible and create a culture that is warn, receptive and respectful of people and their gifts so that they contribute to the company.

We spend over half of our lives at work. Shouldn't we at least have a little fun? Imagine working somewhere that you enjoy. Think of having an environment where growth is recommended and rewarded. How awesome would it be to have a leader that cares not only about the goal of the company, but about you, your goals and your well-being? Wouldn't it be cool to be a part of a culture where vitality is not only in the leader, but in everyone on the team?

Vitality leadership can help with all of this. I know this to be true because I've seen it first-hand in action! Several years ago I worked for a really cool guy who was a fairly new program director at this contracting firm. He and I were working on a project for the federal government. He brought so much life to our team! He made it fun to work again because he helped to create an environment where it was more relaxed but still professional. He would go around from time to time telling corny jokes to ease the pressures of the day. We worked in a data center as we were responsible for creating and maintaining a health website that was used by doctors all over the world.

Every Friday at around 4:30 PM he would round up everyone on the team and say, "Hey!!! It's beer-thirty.....let's go!" Now, we were only able to do this pending there were no outstanding or emergency issues going on at the moment.

He would always have us meet up at this bar and we would be there for about an hour or so just hanging out. Our program director wanted to get to know everyone he worked with a little better. He would ask me how I'm doing with my daughter's soccer team (I was coaching but didn't have a clue the first year). He would also ask my other colleague about her painting endeavors. He would ask where he could find her work so that he could purchase one or two.

He always seemed to know what to say and do which was due to his high emotional intelligence. He just seemed to know when something wasn't right with someone on the team. One morning he dropped by my office to say good morning. I replied in kind but when I did he sensed that I wasn't my ordinary self. He paused for a moment, came back to my office and asked what's really going on. I proceeded to tell him that my daughter (my middle child) wasn't feeling well the night before so I was in and out of sleep all night tending to her every need until she finally fell asleep for good later on that morning.

Once he got the whole story, he proceeded to tell me to finish what I was working on at the moment, and then to leave and go home to get some rest. I was no good to anyone there that day as I was drained from the night before with my daughter and he knew this. He could have just made me stay there and fight my way through it. He could have also just not said anything to me that day. But because of his emotional intelligence and thoughtfulness, his presence in our environment was very much respected and most importantly wanted and needed. His vitality kept us going even when we didn't want to at times.

Small gestures like that earned our trust right away and when he really needed us we would be there with no hesitation. How is vitality leadership playing a part in your professional life?

Let's take another look at vitality leadership from another angle shall we? I took a position years ago working in the internet security field. I had the experience, but was looking for the right opportunity to continue work in that area and possibly grow. The senior director flew into Atlanta, Ga to interview me. The interview went well because I eventually got the position.

I had been in this position for a while and really enjoyed what I was doing. The senior director would work in Atlanta during the week and then fly home on the weekends to Boston, MA. He noticed how well I got along with my teammates and saw that I was able to influence others pretty well. He observed the confidence and trust the others put in me. He pulled me into his office one day and told me what he saw in me the past 4-6 weeks and was wondering if I had ever thought about a leadership position. I told him no at first and that I enjoyed what I was doing but he asked me to think about it more and get back to him.

Several weeks had gone by and he reached out to me once more. He stated that he had to go out of town for a week and asked me to fill in for him in his place while he was out of the office. So we went over a few things in order to prep me for his absence. A week had gone by and he was back in the office bright and early that Monday morning. We had a meeting to go over the week's events so that he was up to speed on where things were.

He asked me how I thought I did while he was out and I explained to him that I felt things went OK. The team was very supportive and there were minor issues that we were able to resolve. He smiled and said, "you sure you don't want to rethink this leadership position again?" I told him I would as he sat there smiling at me.

What he did was a test to get me to see what I could do and how well I could do it. He saw potential, skill and ability in me to lead. He was trying to groom me and empower me to be more than what I was. When I realized this, I sat down with him once more to express my interest in going in a different direction...........leadership. We had a meeting and discussed a career plan with how I would get to that point.

This is part of vitality leadership! He showed that he cared about my growth and my career. He took the time to "introduce me to myself" so to speak. Because I was either too blind to see, or didn't' think it was possible, he had to show me who I was and what I COULD be. He had a hunger for growing people and opening their eyes to different opportunities which in turn gives life to that person or group of people.

Do you, or your team around you have a passion for what you are doing? If not, why? If so, congratulations!! You're almost there!!

The benefits of having vitality leadership and using it effectively

Now that we understand what vitality leadership is and how it can complete and enhance your leadership abilities, let's look at the benefits of it. In order for leaders to positively effect change, empower others, build more leaders, obtain the goal at hand, and pour into others, vitality leadership will have to be implemented successfully because the results or benefits of doing so will create for the leader and the team more **fun, freedom, flexibility and fulfillment**. I know what you're thinking, "how did he get all of that out of vitality leadership?" I'm glad that you asked my friend! Going forward I will break down how you, the leader, can achieve, *"The other side of leadership"* and live a life a bit more pleasing and rewarding like you would like to.

How would you like to have more fun, freedom, flexibility and fulfillment in what you do? We don't think a lot about that in the positions that we're in because we focus so much on the functional leadership. In addition to this, there are others who have been in the position so long, they simply don't want to groom anyone for the future and would rather stay where they are until the inevitable happens. If you want more out of life and out of leadership, continue reading!

QUESTIONS FOR INSIGHT

1. Can you see ways in which vitality leadership can be useful in the way that you lead? How so?

_____

_____

_____

_____

2. What are some ways in which vitality leadership can help you enhance your influence over others?

_____

_____

_____

_____

THE OTHER SIDE OF LEADERSHIP

FUN

Fun is a major benefit of vitality leadership and it's almost to the point where you can't have one without the other! When you or someone who's leading you are constantly providing "life" to the team or to the environment, fun is almost sure to follow because the leader who is the "breath of fresh air" is clearly trying to either create, enhance or reiterate a happy and stress free environment where everyone can come and work and feel relaxed. As I mentioned earlier in the book, we spend so much time at our jobs, shouldn't there be some bit of fun in there as well?

Having fun with what you do is a strong indicator that the temperature for that environment is a very good one! Fun makes people and their surroundings more at ease and therefore those people are able to (and usually do) become more productive than if they didn't have fun at all. Creating fun in your environment can also bring about a level of trust between the leader and the team. The biggest thing about a cohesive, well-run team is the fact that the leader found a way to break down the various negative roadblocks within the team itself. Thus, making them more productive and effective. The vitality leadership that the leader presented was successful in helping everyone find common ground while simultaneously casting the vision and the goal to the team that was put together to achieve it.

When you have fun with what you are doing, and you're able to get everyone around you to have fun as well, little things that used to bother and annoy people suddenly subside. It's no different than if you are on a sports team. As long as you all are winning every week, no one really sweats the small things. The little pesky, irritating things that used to bother you when you were losing no longer matter to you anymore.

27

A lot of times teams have to be shown that just because we're at work, it doesn't mean that we can't somehow make it fun. Other times, it may be the actual team that may have to show the leader the same exact thing! Vitality leadership is a beautiful thing that can give birth to these benefits which can help take the leader to another level.

How many times have you been in a position of leadership and you focused so much on the functional side of things? Many of us believe that because we're adults, we can't have fun at work. We've spent most of our leadership lives working lop-sided! A lot of us are way more on the functional side than the vitality side. Most believe that if you swing more to the vitality side, you aren't serious enough about your work. On the other hand, if you swing more to the functional side, you may be too serious about your work and wound up tighter than a drum!

Everything for the most part should have a balance to it. This alone can be quite the challenge to a leader when it's time for them to jump into action. The following should be a daily or weekly question to yourselves, "Am I having fun with what I'm doing?" I would be so bold as to say that quite a few of us would not like to answer that question because we know in our heart of hearts the answer isn't going to be what we would like for it to be. We've come to the point in life where "fun" is a bad thing at work and that couldn't be further from the truth. When a leader is having fun working with his team, his actions become contagious!

One afternoon I got the opportunity to catch an Atlanta Braves baseball game with some friends of mine after work. It was probably late in the 5th inning when some of us decided to go and grab some food and drinks for everyone. We get to the concessions line and wait patiently until we get to the counter to order. It was there when I saw "fun" live and in the flesh! The owner or the manager of the concession stand was just flying all over the place helping customers and his own team with energy and vigor.

His smile alone could light up an entire room so you could tell he really enjoyed what he was doing and because of that, his team was effected by his actions. You could easily tell because they too were basically mimicking him with their smiles, their energy as well as their customer service to everyone there ordering food. It was amazing to see it in action! His drive and dedication to provide the best experience to the customer he possibly could was evident. His actions were infectious to his team and that's why they were courteous, productive.......and having fun!

Several years ago I had the pleasure of working with this one gentleman who was such a joy to work with! He made it so easy to be around him and was very approachable. If you didn't know any better, you would have sworn that he was one of the guys or part of the actual team. He wasn't though. He was the Director of the IT department for the health company we were working for at the time.

For the sake of the story, we'll call him Mike. Mike's leadership skills were exceptional and was very successful because he had found the balance between the functional leadership and vitality leadership. It was really awesome to work with Mike because he created an environment that was professional but yet relaxed and inviting. Mike brought so much life into our team and environment because he believed much like I do that leadership can be fun and should be fun!

One example is once a week during football season Mike would have us report to the conference room. Usually it would be on a Monday or Tuesday afternoon. During this time frame we would only talk about the football games that took place that prior Sunday or Monday night. It was a way for everyone on the team to bond and connect. We had fun doing it too!

Sometimes Mike would bring everyone together and we'd all go out to lunch together and talk sports. It was his way of strengthening his team and at the same time building a level of trust between him and the team. There were times in the conversations where he would ask questions about us in general. It was awesome to see leadership being genuine because it showed us that we really matter.

These weekly events gave everyone the opportunity to get to know one another a bit more while creating a deeper trust factor with each other. For example, Mike would ask me about how my toastmasters' meetings and how they were going. He would also ask Steve how his wood carving was coming along and that he would definitely love to buy a piece for his wife. These were great moments and it was partially because of these events and others that Mike created for us that made working there and working with each other so much fun!

How much fun are you bringing into your team's environment? Have you even thought about fun in the workplace and how it can benefit both the company and the employees? You set the tone for your group and for the culture of the workplace. Think about ways you can maximize you leadership ability and influence so that you can get the most out of your team. There's nothing wrong with having some fun at work when you go about the right way!

There's a lot to be said about the benefits of having fun where you work. I've read countless articles and blogs about how having fun at work:

- Makes people more focused

- Makes people less fearful of change

- Makes people more productive

- Causes employees to provide excellent customer service

- Boosts everyone's ability to become more creative and think outside of the box

- Creates less "down time"

- Helps minimize absenteeism among employees

- Attracts potential employees

- Provides innovation

I could continue on and on but I believe that you get the picture now. You only live this life once so let's try to make the most of it and expand our leadership and lead with some balance. Every day that we live to see is a gift. Let's take our influence and create a joyful, engaging and productive ideal environment for our team and ourselves.

What are you waiting on!! Start having some fun at work!

QUESTIONS FOR INSIGHT

1. How can you use your vitality leadership skills to incorporate more fun for your team and environment?

_____

_____

_____

_____

2. Can you see the benefits of having fun at work? What other benefits do think can come of having fun in your workplace?

_____

_____

_____

_____

THE OTHER SIDE OF LEADERSHIP

FREEDOM

Vitality leadership can also help bring more freedom to your work and personal life. Most leaders are so deep in the trenches of the work that they rarely have the opportunity to take a few steps back to brainstorm or to see what's coming up on the horizon. Leaders are supposed to lead, cast the vision, see the future, guide the company, and build more leaders but most of them hardly even get that far due to lack of time (and a few other things).

Wouldn't it be nice to have more time to do the things that NEED to be done? Wouldn't it also be nice to have more time to do the things that you WANT to do as well? I can already see you nodding your head yes!

Leaders need freedom in order to regroup at times so that they are able to provide their very best to their team and to the up and coming leaders. Grooming is crucial when it comes to preparing the leaders of tomorrow. Knowing what's coming down the road in 2, 5 or 10 years from now and understanding what it's going to take to keep the company in a competitive advantage takes time and research. However, none of this can happen if you don't have the freedom needed so that you can break away as needed. Freedom can only come to a leader in one way.....**empowerment**!

If we all want the freedom to do the things we need to do and want to do, we have to learn how to educate, train and empower our teams. A lot of leaders want to be "hands on" and in the details of everything but that just drains you and in many ways you are cheating your team. Your team is being cheating out of valuable experiences that you are robbing them from because you feel the need to do it all yourself.

In cases like this, many of your team members will become frustrated and grow tired of not being trusted to do their job. Along with the frustration will eventually come anger and ultimately a deep desire to move on to bigger and better opportunities.

I read an article a while back about a company that was trying to find the best type of manager or leader to promote. The company reviewed two leaders within the same district but at different locations. One leader worked 50-60 hrs a week and had a team but rarely utilized them. If he did, he was over their shoulders until the work was completed. The other leader worked 40hrs a week but he trained and utilized his team. He empowered them to make decisions and gave them room for error while at the same time correcting them and showing them better ways when they were wrong.

Needless to say, the company eventually ended up promoting the leader who worked the 40hr week. Because he was able to train and groom a competent team, he worked 40hrs and had time to do the other things that he needed and wanted to do. The upper management team then asked him if he could train the other leaders in the other districts! Having that freedom gives you the ability to look at the bigger picture and see challenges and opportunities that lie ahead. It allows you time to view things in ways you've never had the chance to see them before.

With more time at your disposal, it can also grant you more time with your family or loved ones. Most of us have grown accustomed to working long hours, weekends, and evenings for the sake of our families and we tend to miss out on some the important moments in life. Having that freedom can afford you the ability to see those soccer games that you missed. Maybe even catch the Spring recital that your daughter is dancing in as the little Sun flower. Finally, you can always score some brownie points with your significant other by getting together for an unexpected lunch date during the week! Nobody and no company is going to care more about your time than you. Think about that!

How awesome would it be to be able to break up the monotony of your day or week with a round of 9 holes at the golf course? If it has to be work related, what about being able to attend a conference that can further assist you in becoming a better leader? These are just some of the things you can accomplish with the freedom that you've created for yourself.

Remember, we're talking about the other side of leadership. There should be a balance that you are always working on trying to perfect. Now, your balance will probably be a little different that someone else's but that's ok. We have to focus on what works for you and helping you to become the best version of yourself that you can possibly be. Time is one of the most precious things in life that can never be replaced or recouped once it's gone. Be wise and work smarter to put yourself in a position so that time is never the enemy, but more so a welcoming friend!

I have a client that I worked with for a while now. She is a Director of Finance for an architecture firm. She wanted assistance on how she could become more effective as a leader and also how she could raise her team's performance. I asked her a series of questions trying to figure out how I would be able to best attack her challenges.

She began to explain how she was very much involved with the team and extremely hands on with them. This method leaves her practically no time to do the things that she needs to do.

She's so bogged down and in the weeds of everything that she's not able to do what great leadership does which is grooming, coaching, inspiring and teaching her team. She's not able to look ahead to see what's trending in their field. She can't research and find the proper resources and materials needed to bring in to help enhance her team's skillset which will make them an even more valuable asset to the organization.

Once I learned this information I asked her if she felt that her team was competent to handle the day to day issues and challenges.

She said, "yes, I believe that they are very capable."

I said, "OK, well what about your team lead? Is he fit to lead and handle the team?"

Again, she said, "Yes, he's great with the team and I trust him completely."

I said, "OK, then LET HIM LEAD!" I added, "you don't pay smart, competent people a lot of money to control them and tell them what to do."

I had to explain to her that even though it was her team, she had to get to a point where she empowers her team lead to actually lead the team and make the right calls. In addition to this, she had to let go of the team and empower them to work together and work with the team lead to formulate the best resolutions to their problems.

She had to learn to let go and allow them to be held accountable for what they do. They should only come to you if it's something that they just can't seem to agree on or actually needs your blessing to continue. Once she was able to get to that place, freedom gladly greeted her!

With this new found freedom that she has acquired, I then worked with her on what she felt could be gained from having this freedom. How could she use it to her advantage professionally and personally? Professionally, she could look for the appropriate training and tools that she felt her team needed in order to tackle the challenges of today and the future. She also looked at conferences that they all could attend that would give them immediate valuable information that would greatly enhance their skillset and productivity.

On a personal level, she had more time and freedom to go out and have lunch with a client and not have to decline so much because she was so involved like she was earlier. She knew that it was "bad business" to constantly cancel and reschedule but at that time she didn't know then what she knows now. This new freedom also allowed her to take care of other personal matters that normally would have to wait until late in the evening or on weekends.

As you can see, you can use the freedom that you have created for yourself in a myriad of ways that are constructive both professionally and personally. Freedom gives you the opportunity to deal with the dynamics of your job and of life itself. Needless to say that my client was very excited with the newly acquired freedom she had obtained. She was so wise with the use of it that it was impressive to her senior management and within six months she was promoted!

When she learned how to get more freedom on her job, she turned around and used it to make herself and her team better. She also used it to accomplish other tasks that her piers claimed to be too busy to tackle. She showed wisdom and creativity with her extra time and it paid off for her.

This new-found freedom also paid off for the team lead and the team as well. The lead was excited about being in control without my client always over their shoulder. His confidence had grown and the team responded very well to his leadership and competency. The productivity and the morale of the team was very high and they truly appreciated being given the chance to perform without the oversight of my client.

Having freedom can pay off for you as well. The neat thing about it is, you get to determine how it will pay off for you! If you're having a hard time meeting goals and objectives because you are too involved in the team's daily activities, learn how to train, empower and let them go! It is only then that you will reach another level of leadership and accountability. If you happen to be your own boss, freedom gives you the advantage to go out and attract new business!

The freedom itself doesn't guarantee that you'll be successful, but it's what you do with it that determines your happiness and success!

Go get free today!!

QUESTIONS FOR INSIGHT

1. How important is freedom to you in leadership? How do you plan to use it?

_____

_____

_____

_____

2. Is freedom imperative to you in order to lead effectively? Why?

_____

_____

_____

_____

Flexibility

Now this is probably one of the biggest things that people are looking for now when they are either seeking employment or in leadership as well. However, freedom gives you the capacity to be flexible or to have flexibility. Flexibility allows you wiggle room in life to modify, update, and/or change whatever it is you need to. It has become somewhat of a "deal breaker" for a lot of millennials that are coming up into the work force now and companies are having to modernize their way of doing business. In recent years, flexibility has become a way of life due to the fact that our lives are much more dynamic than ever before.

Imagine that as a leader, you are seeing things that your company really needs to start thinking about and planning for. Or maybe you are noticing that with some updated training, your team or department can be ahead of the game and take their service and productivity to another level. Well, having the flexibility to plan, coordinate and execute the things that need to be in place for your team to succeed is crucial and much needed. Take some time to think about how you can better serve your team, company, or most importantly, your family with flexibility.

One of the best feelings in the world is being able to have your son or daughter look out into the crowd and see you there supporting them. This was allowed because you had the flexibility to leave work early, attend the event and support your child, and then finish up work later on that evening. Flexibility allows you to do more in life as well as get more out of life. It also gives you the capability to increase your productivity regardless if it's work or personal related.

One major contributor to flexibility is technology. We live in an age now where we can be almost anywhere at any time and do what we need to do because we now have the means to it with. With technology, we can hold virtual meetings with several people from across the globe in the comfort of our homes (and even in our pajamas!). We can send an important message instantly across oceans and mountains within a matter of seconds! Technology gives flexibility life and value.

Think about this, you have to pick up your kids from after school care by 3PM. At the very same time, you also have this very important meeting that you must attend via conference call. You no longer have to stay chained to a physical chair and desk in order to take the call. You can be in your car driving to the school while jumping on the conference call on your cell phone.

Another good example of flexibility is the issue that one of my co-workers had a few years back when his son had become suddenly ill at school. His son's temperature had spiked and he had been throwing up at school. My co-worker got the call from the school's nurse about his son and was asked to come pick him up.

This could not have come at a worse time because my co-worker was working on a deadline of the following morning. Now, long ago he would have been in a situation where he would have had to leave work and go grab his son, take him home or to a relative's house, and then go back to work for the rest of the evening until his work was done.

With the flexibility that we have today, he can take his laptop and his son and go home. He can work on nursing his son back to health while working on his project all in the comfort of his house and all due to the flexibility that we have today.

My wife was recently in a situation where her work hours wouldn't allow her the ability to see our daughter's soccer and basketball games. This was really hard on her and the girls because she wanted to be there and the girls certainly wanted to see their mom there as well. After a while she decided to have a chat with her leadership and was able to work out an alternative work schedule. She would be able to go in earlier so that she could get off earlier. This worked out great for all of us all because her leadership was flexible and allowed for this change to happen. Now, mom and the girls are happy and these one in a lifetime moments can be seen and treasured!

Flexibility is important because it allows you the opportunity to accommodate your family, customers, clients and organization. Clients and employees acquire a level of trust with you because you are able to make yourself available and cater to their needs. If you don't have any flexibility today, I would strongly urge you to find a way to get it and incorporate it into your leadership role.

The benefits far outweigh the cons!

QUESTIONS FOR INSIGHT

1. How do you see flexibility working to your advantage in your professional and personal life?

_____

_____

_____

_____

2. What does flexibility look like in your environment? Would you consider it a "must-have" in order to improve your leadership? Why?

_____

_____

_____

_____

THE OTHER SIDE OF LEADERSHIP

Fulfillment

There are 86,400 seconds in a day, no more and no less. On an average life span of 76 years, you spend between 20-35% of your life working. Now, as I said earlier on, we spend quite a bit of time at work on a daily basis. If that's the case, shouldn't we try to incorporate a little more fun, freedom, flexibility and fulfillment? Looking at the rough estimate that I just gave you about time in a day and how much of it we spend working during our life span, do you have fulfillment in what you are doing?

In other words, are you achieving what you've desired at work? Do you feel that you are making a difference where you are? A lot of people work jobs that anger, frustrate, confuse, depress and paralyze them. Most people would leave their jobs today if they were somehow able to do so. Why is that? Some feel that they weren't fully briefed on all of their job responsibilities or duties. Others feel that their boss is incompetent and most times not even qualified to lead. However, most people don't like their jobs and would leave them if they could because they aren't fulfilling.

As leaders, we have to understand that people want to feel a part of something greater than themselves. They want to feel included and have their voice acknowledged and their work appreciated. Are you doing what you like to do? Is what you do fulfilling to you? If so, great! If not, why? More importantly, why are you still there? If we're completely honest here, many of us sacrifice fulfillment for a false sense of happiness in what is called, a paycheck. We place more value in the income that we receive every week or every two weeks than we do in our own selves and our need for being fulfilled .

Don't get me wrong, I do understand the necessity of receiving an income. However, if money is all that you are chasing, it's also something you will never have enough of. When money is the only motivator, your passions take a back seat to your life and you'll become one of those people on an endless journey. I call it the endless journey because the more you make, the more you'll want. On the other hand, when you are going after your passion, you are actually going after fulfillment. Being fulfilled means that you happy with what you are doing, how you are doing it, and why you are doing it.

I used to be one of those people who chased the money because I thought that was the most important at that time. I would work as a contractor on an assignment for a while and when a friend or an old colleague of mine would share some insight on another contract for more money, I would jump at it. I did this for a while when I got a wakeup call from a dear friend of mine. He asked me if I enjoyed what I did. I responded by saying that it was OK but that the money is excellent.

I was young at the time but he really got me to thinking about my wants and desires. He went on to ask me if I was excited about what I did or was my passion in what I was doing. WOW!!! I had never thought about that. Am I happy with what I'm doing? That's when I realized that I was on an endless journey. I had the money but no fulfillment. I was "existing" in life instead of "living" life.

I really had to sit down and re-evaluate what I was doing and why. The money gave me a false sense of security and I didn't realize it. I was content working on contracts as a mindless puppet as long as the money was good. Big mistake! You look up 5,10,15yrs later and wonder where all of the time went. Years are lost because money solely over being fulfilled.

I know of a young man who works as a waiter in a fancy New Orleans restaurant for about 5yrs now and he enjoys every day of it! Now, of course he could have gone back to school and eventually landed a really great job with some corporation but he chose the profession of a waiter. He enjoys serving others and creating a wonder experience for all of his customers. He receives enormous amounts of praise and recognition for service. Most importantly, if you ask him why he likes his job so much, he'll tell you that it's very fulfilling to him.

Another great example is a young lady who left her career as a prominent lawyer to become a waitress at a diner. I know what you are thinking but just hear me out. She had a very demanding boss who never respected her no matter how well she did her job. She was very well compensated but completely over-worked and underappreciated. After several years of this, she eventually quit her job and took up a position as a waitress at a local dine.

She gets asked all the time why would she do something like that. She could have easily gone to another law firm and continued her life in law. She just smiles and says that she found another way to serve and help people. She can do this without all the rudeness, politics, and sexual harassment. The biggest reason why she likes the change is because it is so fulfilling to her to serve people in this manner AND.........people are more apt to say a simple "Thank you!" for my services. WHO WOULD HAVE THOUGHT RIGHT!! When you are doing what you feel gives you purpose, your work is effortless, you're a lot more happier, and your productivity is always higher than average.

We put ourselves at a disadvantage daily when we aren't giving our best to what we do. When we aren't fulfilled or doing things that are fulfilling, we only cheat ourselves and everyone around us. Lack of skill, enthusiasm, purpose and knowledge of the job are just a few things that can cause us to feel unfulfilled. Lack of education can also contribute heavily to you being unfulfilled. I used to be a contractor for a health government agency many years ago. I was an application engineer and even though I loved working in I.T., I just felt like what I was doing at that time was meaningless. Needless to say my work was mediocre and I did what I needed to do just to get by day after day.

One day while in the server room configuring servers to be added to the network, I got the opportunity to chat with one of the directors of my projects. Over lunch we started talking about his project and what it was specifically about. After becoming educated about his project and how important it was to third world countries and doctors abroad, it was now clear why what I did on that project was so crucial. I had finally become fulfilled in what I was doing. I had a purpose now and understood what it meant to have the technology in place to help save lives. I always liked helping people in any way that I could and now I could see directly how my work was impacting others in a positive way.

Leaders, it doesn't matter in what capacity you lead in, just make sure that your work is fulfilling to you. When you are doing work that's fulfilling, you do it with the best of your ability. You do it with a sense of pride and respect. The director helped educate me on why what I did was so important to the project. Most people (like myself at the time) didn't understand where we fit in on the big cog wheel of the project or company. We need to explain to our teams what important role they play within the many pieces to the puzzle of an organization.

Fulfillment is like a level of completeness to any human being. As leaders we need to understand that in order to obtain fulfillment in work and in life, we need to know our "why". Why is it that we do what we do? Why am I working here?

Once you spend time thinking about these things and formulating your answers, think about asking your team the same thing. Are they feeling fulfilled? Do they know their "why"? You don't want people around that are only there to collect a check. You want a team that has and knows their purpose and has an interest in achieving the goal at hand.

Fulfillment should be at the forefront of your mind any and every time you embark upon a job or a challenge. It should be the "paycheck" that we seek. It is only then that your hopes and dreams, once obtained, will give you a feeling of completeness.

QUESTIONS FOR INSIGHT

1. How are you fulfilled in the leadership role that you are in now? If not fulfilled, how do you plan to go about it?

   _____

   _____

   _____

   _____

2. Is fulfillment the ultimate form of success for you? If so, how so? If not, why not?

   _____

   _____

   _____

   _____

S.M.A.R.T GOALS FOR VITALITY LEADERSHIP

I wanted to add a bonus here to help you get started with implementing vitality leadership where ever you are! First, we must understand the S.M.A.R.T methodology....

S = Specific
M= Measurable
A=Achievable
R=Relevance
T=Timely

In order to be successful, we need to figure out a way to use this methodology in order to map out how we should implement vitality leadership and get the best results and impact. We're going to go step-by-step with some examples so that you are clear on what you need to do.

After you take some time to complete this exercise, you should have a well-documented plan on how you will attack this challenge. Remember, it's a living, breathing document so should you need to change anything, it won't be a problem. We just want to make sure that you have the best plan possible for your success! Let's begin!!

The "S" is for Specific

OK, let's be specific about our goal(s) for implementing vitality leadership. What exactly are we trying to accomplish using vitality leadership. Below are a few examples that you can either use for yourself, or as a guide.

I want to implement vitality leadership because………..

- I want to enhance my leadership ability and influence.

- I want to have better employee/employer engagements with my team and improve the working environment

- I want to have a relaxed environment and consistent high productivity.

You can use any or all of those or create your own below

Write in your specific goal below:

I want to implement vitality leadership because:

_____

_____

The "M" is for Measurable

We now have to figure out how we're going to measure our success of implementing vitality leadership. Now this can be tricky and somewhat of a challenge. Below is an example of how I believe we can measure your success.

I can measure the success of my implementation of vitality leadership by.....

- noticing how fast my influence and leadership ability has grown.

- how quickly the employer/employee engagements have improved with the team.

- Seeing how relaxed the environment is now and the increased productivity.

In other words, take note of the current conditions and situations and document it. Next, start your implementation process for vitality leadership and document the positive changes you see and how soon you see them.

You can use any or all of those or create your own below

Write in your specific goal below:

I'm going to measure the success of my implementation of vitality leadership by:

_____

_____

The "A" is for Achievable

Next, we need to figure out if our goal(s) is achievable. In this situation it is a resounding YES!!!!

This step should be fairly easy. We are basically asking ourselves if this be done. Review your specific goals and how you plan to measure them. If you feel that those are legitimate and able to accomplish, you should be in pretty good shape!

We always want to set up goals that are achievable or realistic.

The "R" is for Relevance

We're almost done! We need to look and see if our goals support the company's objectives. Frankly speaking, are your goals in line with what the company wants or is expecting of you and your team? Honestly, there's no reason why they can't line up to what the company wants. Remember, this is a living and breathing document!!

If you want, you can write out or explain how your goal(s) are relevant to the company's objectives. It would be good to be able to write out and explain how what you are doing aligns with what the company wants.

Explain your relevance below:

_____

_____

_____

_____

The "T" is for Time bound

This is the last one! What we want to do now is to estimate or give ourselves a time frame as to when we think we will see the results or changes based upon our implementation of vitality leadership. It's about like project management. When you're managing a project regardless if it's a project around the house or if it's work related, you want to know roughly about how much time it will take to complete it.

Our lives are built and exist around time so it's very important to us how much time something will take to complete. In this case, it can vary based on many, many dynamics that make up your environment that you want to change. As in the step before this one, be realistic in your estimated time that you set to effectively implement vitality leadership. The best thing about this is that there is no good or bad time frame to target. We just want to make sure that we implement correctly so that the effects and results are what we expected.

For the sake of completing this S.M.A.R.T goal method, we could use the following:

I plan to see a complete turnaround in my leadership skills, environment, productivity and employee/employer engagement in about 6 months.

Again, this is just an example. It may take you and your situation a little longer or shorter.

Write your time bound statement below:

I plan to see _____

_____

in about _____ .

Conclusion

This book was written with the intention of introducing people to a side of leadership that exists but yet is unknown (or at the very least not spoken about). The significance of this book is really just breaking down both sides of leadership and showing you why it's important as well as how.

Year after year I see leaders step into their positions and fail miserably because they have this preconceived idea that leadership is just a one-way street. They were never taught that how you lead has to be dynamic and fluid. Therefore, their leadership becomes a liability because they don't know how to use it. Not only do your goals and objectives matter, but people matter too.

I think this would be a good time to add that with the vitality side of leadership, you mostly get out of it what you put into it. I say this mostly because there are times when you go about trying to become the vital force in your environment, but you still end up with one or more people who just don't want to change. In that case, it may be best to reel the outcasts in to see why there's resistance. Sometimes the ultimate choice is to modify the team in order to be successful.

You have to remember that when you start to incorporate the vitality side of leadership, it will require buy-in to a certain extent. In other words, you're showing them what they can have and how the environment and culture can be. At the same time, you're also showing them what you need and why you need it, as well as the benefits of having it. And what is the need again? Fun, Freedom, Flexibility, and Fulfillment!

I enjoy showing people what's necessary for them to do in order to master acquiring their balance in leadership. I work hard with my clients in order to transform them into "life - givers" regardless of the environment or industry they work in. When leaders succeed, the people around should succeed as well.

After reading this book, you should at least understand both sides and how to utilize them to better your leadership skills as well as your personal life. Balance brings peace and stability. When people that are working for you see and experience the balance, they too will want the same thing at work and in life! A happy and balanced environment equals productivity and success!!

THE AUTHOR

Chad D. Bumgarner
www.Chadbumgarner.co

ABOUT THE AUTHOR

Chad is one of the most upbeat and passionate speakers out today but he's so much more than that. He is also a team - building facilitator and a leadership development coach with the background and experience to help leaders knock down mental blinders so that they can see what's holding them back.

Chad has spent years speaking to hundreds of people about how to become a more effective and impactful leader. He understands the importance of balance when it comes to leadership and leading people.

Chad is committed to reaching as many people as he can so that he can help them become addicted to the process of progress. He wants people to lead with passion and get the most out of life and leadership!

"Speaking and leadership development coaching are both passions of mine." They both are a gateway to my happiness! I enjoy helping leaders enhance their leadership abilities so that they can become the leader that people WANT to follow! In order for this to happen, it's crucial that they learn the vitality side of leadership so that they too can experience the fun, freedom, flexibility & fulfillment that it provides.

If you want Chad to coach you, hold a training session, or even come out to speak at an event, please inquire about his availability as well as other specific services you would like for him to provide at *info@chadbumgarner.co*

"If your actions inspire others to dream more, learn more, do more and become more, you are a leader."

- John Quincy Adams

Other Writings by
Chad D. Bumgarner

CHAD'S PLAYBOOK TO EFFECTIVE LEADERSHIP

The book is meant to take mediocre or good leaders and turn them into better, more effective leaders.

2015©
ISBN 9-780692-519349

Available now at **amazon.com** and **createspace.com**

<u>NOTES</u> :

THE OTHER SIDE OF LEADERSHIP